THE REALLY BIG BARN
ON NOAH'S FARM

Darrell Wiskur

The Really Big Barn

On Noah's Farm

First printing: August 2001

Illustrations and story by Darrell Wiskur

ISBN: 0-89051-353-8
Library of congress: 2001091164

Printed in the United States of America

For information write:
Master Books, Inc.
P.O. Box 727
Green Forest, AR 72638

For other great titles visit our web site at:
www.masterbooks.net

For publicity information contact Dianna Fletcher at
1-870-438-5288

Master Books

T is an old story and, yes, it is true
Of Noah, his kin, and a big floating zoo.
The rest of that story is chock full of charm
As old Noah's ark became Noah's barn.

The flood was over, the waters had crested;
And up on the mount the ark came and rested.
The mud from the flood by now was all dried,
And Noah was ready to move on outside.

God said to Noah, "Come out of the ark,
With all of these creatures and make a new start.
The ark door was opened and Noah stepped out,
Held up his hands and gave a great shout.

Then with rumbling and rattling and clicking and clacking
And clucking and mooing and cooing and quacking,
The birds and the beasts and the creatures galore
Came trotting and tripping
right out of the door.

The men searched for stones as the land became drier.

An altar they built for a sacrifice fire.

Offerings were made by the men and their wives.

They thanked God and praised Him for saving their lives.

And God was pleased with what they had done.

He gladly blessed Noah and all of his sons.

He gave them instructions to show them their worth,

"Be fruitful, increase — replenish the earth."

That day on the mountain, viewing his farm,

Noah's great ark became his great barn.

Some creatures would stay — those that were mild;

The others would leave to live in the wild.

God split up the animals that very day:

"Horses and chickens and cattle can stay.

But monkeys and mongoose, coyotes and crow,

Leopards and llamas and lynxes must go."

In the really big barn, they stored lots of seed.
Some was for planting; some was for feed.
They stored bushels of barley, rye, wheat, and oats,
To make bread for their table, and food for the goats.

E ach spring Noah's family planted the farm,
with provisions they stored in the really big barn.
In the fields they sowed seeds of all different kinds,
And set out the vineyards from cuttings of vines.

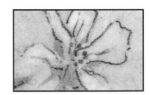

Cows were part of God's great plan.
Cows were specially made for man.
By the barn, the cows would stay.
The little calves would romp and play.

The cows were milked; the milk was good.
In shade they laid and chewed their cud.
With cows and goats, the really big barn
Turned into the really big dairy farm!

Now, about the rain,
Ducks won't complain
And geese will dash
To splish and splash.

But hens just sigh
They like it dry
They sneer with clucks
At geese and ducks

Who piddle and dawdle
And paddle and waddle
And must be insane
To stay in the rain!

There's no time to play
With more eggs to lay
So, cozy and warm,
Hens stay out of the storm.

With blessings of God, old Noah's farm grew.

And his flocks and his herds, his whole family, too!

Orchards and vineyards and groves and great fields,

Did help the farm prosper with bountiful yields.

T

The work was real hard, not lightweight or breezy,
To build a great farm has never been easy.
They all worked together; the work never slowed.
The strong beasts of burden carried the load.

Many children were born and numbers increased,

Soon houses were needed; the work never ceased.

The ark had been made, right from the start,

To be used again — be taken apart.

The lumber was used to build some new houses,

For Noah, his wife, their sons and their spouses.

With ample supplies — rocks, labor, and sand,

Buildings sprang up all over the land.

There were nieces and nephews,

aunts, uncles and cousins,

Grandmas and grandpas and babies by dozens.

Too many there were, so in groups they went forth,

And went to make farms all over the earth.

So that's how it started, how the new world began
God saw it was good and He blessed the land.
Because Noah was faithful, and Noah obeyed,
God used him and blessed him and gave him His aid.

Noah grew many crops, many crops very tall,
But one single crop was the choicest of all.
Twasn't bushels of barley or wheat in the carts,
But the love of the Lord that grew in their hearts.

Chickens are common worldwide. Their eggs are a staple food to every farmer's diet. They like to chase bugs and scratch and peck around for food. The rooster (male) is well known for his "cock-a-doodle-doo" at sunrise.

Cattle need a lot of space in which to graze and they prefer well-watered grasslands to scrub country. Cattle provide a good volume of products to the farmer in meat, milk, cheese, and leather.

Camels are known as "the ship of the desert" because they can walk for long distances across the desert sand toting 500 pounds on their backs, going far before they need to stop for water.

NOAH'S FAVORITE

Ducks spend most of their time in water. They bob and dive, dip and shiver, shake, splash and chase. Baby ducks stay close to mom and peep to her as they follow her through the water. Ducks give a generous supply of quality feather down and large eggs.

Since Noah's time **horses** have been developed to become one of man's most versatile animal helpers and have been bred to fit many different roles: kings' war horses, parade horses, cow ponies, or plow horses.

Donkeys are hard working, evenly dispositioned creatures. They are strong and sure-footed, which makes them good pack animals. Because of their size and gentle spirit they make excellent working companions to their masters.

Sheep are desirable for farms because they need less food and space than cattle; they are a food source for rich milk and cheese; and their wool is spun into yarn to make wool cloth.

FARM CRITTERS

Although they look somewhat similar, **geese** are larger than ducks, more protective of their territory and family, and lay huge eggs. Goose down is superior for insulating clothes and bedding.

Sparrows are common to almost any place that has a growing season. Although not a domestic creature, sparrows love being near people and like to use man-made structures for nesting. Their natural diet includes insects and seeds from wild flowers or grains.

Some **goats** are ornery; some are friendly, but each one has its own separate personality. They will pull at and nibble on anything within their climbing or stretching reach. Goats love to climb and will run, jump and pounce over the roughest terrain.

Ark Construction

The ark could have made a really big barn. Noah built the ark to God's specifications. Genesis 6 describes the size of the ark as 450 feet long, 75 feet wide, and 45 feet high. It had three floors and a door in the side. Included in the design was an 18-inch tall window that wrapped around the top floor. There were rooms throughout the ark, and the wood used for its construction was gopher wood, which Noah sealed inside and out with pitch (Genesis 6:14).

The logs Noah had available were from trees many hundreds of years old, which could have grown to giant proportions in a pre-flood environment, much different than growing conditions we know today. The ark was skillfully designed and constructed and could have been put together without nails, slot fitted and locked with removable dowel pins so that it could be dismantled for portability of pre-fabricated sections. This would make it totally efficient for building construction material later.

About the Author

Darrell Wiskur has enjoyed working as an artist for over thirty years. He is the illustrator and author of the Master Books children's title, Timothy Whale's Rainbow.

His illustrations have been recognized by the New York Society of Illustrators and his book designs have won print awards. As a designer, he holds numerous patents and copyrights on toys, games, and fishing equipment.

Darrell lives with his wife Patricia in Harrison, Arkansas. They are the parents of seven children and grandparents of thirteen grandchildren.